Disney's

TOONTOWN

A Very Merry Christmas Alphabet

XMAS LIGHTS

Written by Margaret Snyder

Illustrated by Phil Ortiz

MERRIGOLD PRESS • NEW YORK

©1994 The Walt Disney Company. All rights reserved. Printed in the U.S.A. No part of this book may be reproduced or copied in any form without written permission from the copyright owner. MERRIGOLD PRESS® AND MERRIGOLD PRESS & DESIGN™ are the property of Merrigold Press, New York, New York 10022. Library of Congress Catalog Card Number: 94-78276 ISBN: 0-307-10977-1 A MCMXCIV

A

is for **Aprons**, they keep us so neat!

is for **Bells** we hear on the street.

3

C is for Christmas **Cards** spreading good cheer.

is for **December,** the best time of the year!

E is for **Elves** painting dollies and drums.

F is for **Fairies**, who make sugarplums.

G is for **Garland.**

H is for **Holly.**

is for **Icicle.** Isn't that jolly!

9

J is for **Jam** to eat with a spoon.

K is for **Kisses** for every good Toon!

L is for **Lights**, strung with great care.

XMAS LIGHTS

M is for **Mistletoe.** Donald, beware!

N is for **Night,** so clear and so cold.

O is for **Ornaments,** red, green, and gold.

15

P is for **Presents** piled under the tree.
Do you think you can guess
what each one might be?

Q is for **Quilts** piled high on the bed.

18

R is for **Reindeer** that fly overhead.

19

S is for **Stockings,** all hung up with care,
full of Christmastime treats for good Toons to share.

T is for **Top,** another new toy.

U is for **Unwrap.** Oh, what a joy!

is for **Visitors** with goodies galore.

is for **Wreath** hung up on the door.

X is for **Xylophone,** whose sound is so sprightly.

Y is for **Yule** log, burning hotly and brightly.

23

Z is for **Z-Z-Z-Z's** as the Toons soundly sleep, dreaming of Christmas. *Shhh.* Don't make a peep!

24